Library of Congress Control Number: 2011925167

ISBN 978-93-8982-394-3

First edition, September 2011
Edited by Cassandra Pelham
Creative Director: David Saylor
Book Design by Phil Falco and Kazu Kibuishi

This Edition: November 2022

Printed in India

KAZU KIBUISHI

BOOK FOUR
THE LAST COUNCIL

AN IMPRINT OF
■SCHOLASTIC

NEW YORK   TORONTO   LONDON   AUCKLAND   SYDNEY   MEXICO CITY   NEW DELHI   HONG KONG

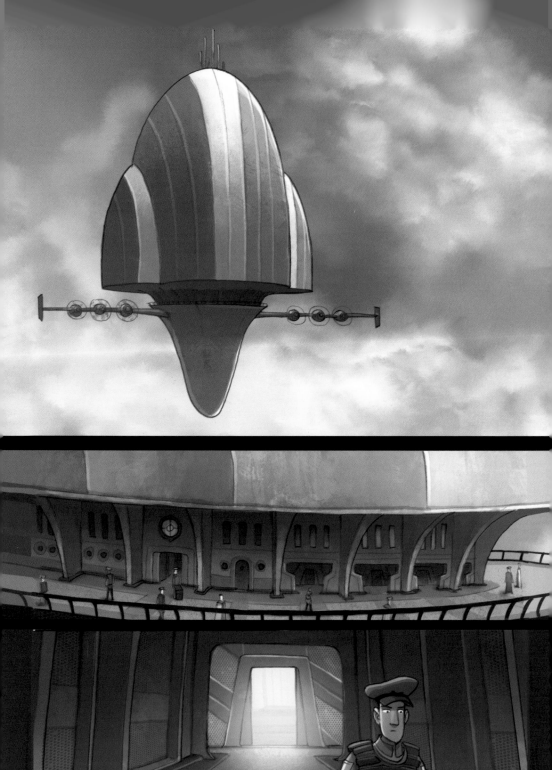

IT'S BETTER THAT YOU DO NOT KNOW.
WHY KEEP SECRETS FROM ME?
I'M YOUNG, BUT THAT DOESN'T MEAN I DON'T KNOW WHAT I'M DOING.
YOU ARE NOT READY.
FWOOSH!

NOT YET. YOU WILL BE SOON.
WHEN YOU BEGIN TO REALIZE THE TRUE WEIGHT OF YOUR ACTIONS...
...YOU WILL AWAKEN TO BECOME THE PERSON THIS WORLD NEEDS YOU TO BE.

WE'LL BE TAKING THE DROPSHIPS INTO THE CITY. YOUR FAMILY AND FRIENDS ARE ALREADY BOARDING.

THEIR SHIP IS FULL, SO YOU WILL BE RIDING WITH ME.

WATCH YOUR STEP.

I DON'T TRUST THESE GUYS, MOM.

I STILL DON'T SEE WHY THEY HAD TO TAKE TRELLIS AND LUGER PRISONER.

I'M SURE THEY HAVE THEIR REASONS.

THEY KNOW MORE THAN WE DO, NAVIN.

YOUR MOM'S RIGHT, KID.

YOU DON'T KNOW SQUAT.

BUT TRELLIS AND LUGER ARE OUR FRIENDS!

IF THERE'S ONE THING I'VE LEARNED IN MY LIFE, IT'S THAT YOU CAN NEVER TRUST AN ELF.

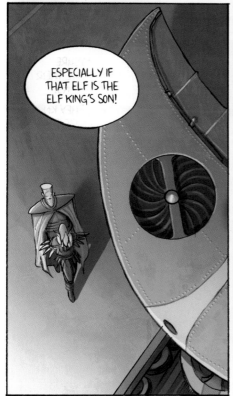

ESPECIALLY IF THAT ELF IS THE ELF KING'S SON!

THE OTHERS ARE READY FOR TRANSPORT, SIR.

THANK YOU, LEN.

TELL DUNCAN WE'RE READY AS WELL.

YES, SIR.

THESE MEN, THEY TREAT YOU LIKE YOU'RE THEIR LEADER.

WHY?

MY FATHER WAS CAPTAIN OF THE CIELIS GUARD.

I TOOK HIS PLACE WHEN HE PASSED AWAY.

SO I'M THE CAPTAIN UNTIL THE COUNCIL DECIDES ON A REPLACEMENT.

I HAVE TO ADMIT THAT POLICE WORK NEVER REALLY SUITED ME.

MY REAL AMBITION IS TO BE ON THE COUNCIL.

IT SHOULD BE YOUR GOAL, TOO.

WHY?

TO HAVE THE ABILITY TO MAKE A DIFFERENCE, OF COURSE.

AND THE COUNCIL WILL DETERMINE WHO AMONG US DESERVES TO HAVE IT.

AND HOW WILL THEY DECIDE?

THROUGH A SERIES OF TESTS.

TO PASS, ALL WE WILL NEED TO DO IS SURVIVE.

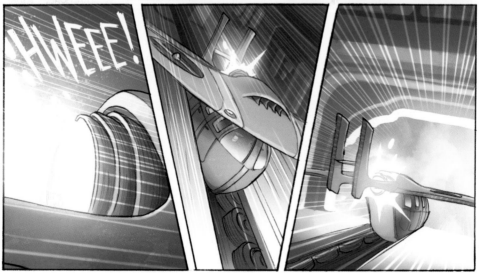

HWEEE!

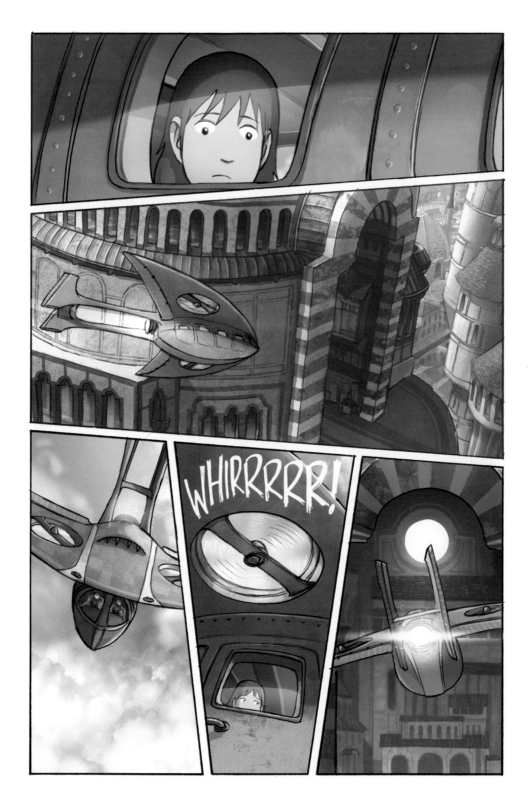

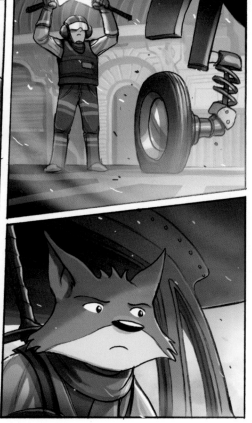

YOU ARE NOT AUTHORIZED TO GO BEYOND THIS POINT.

BUT I'M WITH THEM.

ONLY STONE-KEEPERS AND THEIR FAMILIES ARE ALLOWED ACCESS TO THE ACADEMY.

BUT I WAS ORDERED BY THE GUARDIAN COUNCIL TO DELIVER THE STONEKEEPER MYSELF.

DO YOU HAVE PAPERWORK?

HEY, LEON --

PAPERWORK?

LET ME SPEAK TO YOUR SUPERIOR!

JUST LET IT GO.

24

WHAT ARE WE SUPPOSED TO DO, THEN?

WHAT HAPPENS TO US?

YOU'RE RELIEVED OF YOUR DUTIES.

JUST ENJOY YOUR TIME IN CIELIS.

I SUGGEST BEGINNING BY TAKING A WALK.

YOU KNOW WHAT?

THAT SOUNDS LIKE A GREAT IDEA.

C'MON, LEON.

THERE'S SOMETHING WRONG WITH THIS PICTURE, ENZO.

SOMETHING'S AMISS.

HEY, LOOK, THOSE YAHOOS WON'T RUIN MY TIME HERE.

AND NEITHER WILL YOU.

NOW SHOW US WHERE TO FIND SOME GOOD FOOD AROUND HERE!

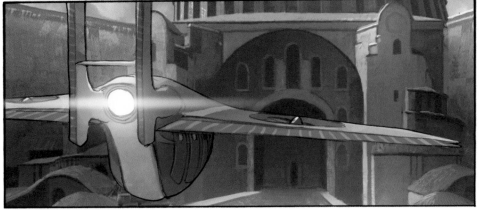

26

WELCOME TO YARBORO PRISON.

A LITTLE BIRD TOLD ME THAT YOU ARE THE SON OF THE DEVIL HIMSELF.

WHEN I HEARD THAT THE ELF KING WAS YOUR FATHER, I ASKED TO BE IN CHARGE OF YOU, PERSONALLY.

NOW, YOU SHOULD KNOW THAT MY FAMILY WAS KILLED BY YOUR PEOPLE BACK IN THE WAR.

AND I'M THE KIND OF MAN WHO DOESN'T FORGET THINGS TOO EASILY.

THIS IS QUITE A VIEW!

THE BEST IN THE CITY, MA'AM.

YOUR DAUGHTER IS BEING GIVEN THE OPPORTUNITY OF A LIFETIME, MRS. HAYES.

VERY FEW STONE-KEEPERS ARE GIVEN THIS CHANCE.

I HATE TO SOUND IGNORANT, BUT WHAT EXACTLY IS THIS "CHANCE" THAT'S BEING PRESENTED TO EMILY?

IF SHE IS IN FACT WHO THE COUNCIL HAS BEEN LOOKING FOR,

THEN SHE MIGHT JUST HELP US SAVE THE WORLD.

IT IS WHERE THE MOST POWERFUL STONEKEEPERS IN HISTORY HELD COURT.

THIS IS THE GRAND HALL OF THE ACADEMY.

AND NOW WE'LL HAVE THE OPPORTUNITY TO JOIN THEIR RANKS.

MAX, IS THIS THE GUARDIAN COUNCIL'S CHAMBER?

YES.

HOW DO I GET INSIDE?

WE NEED TO SPEAK WITH THEM.

I'M SORRY, EMILY.

THAT'S NOT HOW THINGS WORK AROUND HERE.

YOU CAN'T SIMPLY GO AND BOTHER THEM UNANNOUNCED.

WE DON'T HAVE TIME FOR THIS, MAX!

WE NEED TO TELL THEM ABOUT THE ELF KING BEFORE IT'S TOO LATE!

AND YOU DON'T THINK THEY ALREADY KNOW?

THE GUARDIAN COUNCIL KNOWS EVERYTHING.

YOU WILL HAVE YOUR AUDIENCE WITH THEM.

BUT YOU MUST BE PATIENT.

NOW FOLLOW ME.

I'LL SHOW YOU TO YOUR NEW LIVING QUARTERS.

THIS MUST BE A MISTAKE.

THIS PLACE IS JUST SO... SO FANCY.

I ASSURE YOU THIS IS NO MISTAKE.

YOUR DAUGHTER IS ALREADY HELD IN VERY HIGH ESTEEM HERE IN CIELIS.

I DON'T LIKE THIS PLACE, EM.

WHERE ELSE CAN WE GO, NAVIN?

THESE PEOPLE ARE SUPPOSED TO BE THE ONLY ONES WHO CAN HELP US.

I ALWAYS THOUGHT WE WERE ON OUR OWN.

YOU NEED TO BEGIN TAKING THIS OPPORTUNITY A LITTLE MORE SERIOUSLY, EMILY.

AND ONLY THE STRONGEST WILL EARN THE RIGHT TO LEAD OUR ARMY AGAINST THE ELF KING.

THESE TESTS DETERMINE WHO AMONG US ARE THE STRONGEST STONEKEEPERS.

IT IS YOUR DUTY TO HELP US HOWEVER YOU CAN.

NOW, MAKE SURE YOU GET PLENTY OF REST TONIGHT.

YOU'RE GOING TO NEED IT.

HAVE A GOOD EVENING, MRS. HAYES.

GOOD NIGHT, MAX.

SHUT.

HE SEEMS NICE.

WE HAVE TO GET OUT OF HERE AND FIND THE OTHERS.

KCHNK KCHNK

IT'S LOCKED.

CAN'T YOU JUST BLAST THROUGH IT WITH THE STONE?

NO.

EVER SINCE WE ENTERED THE ACADEMY GROUNDS, THE STONE'S POWER HAS FELT SO WEAK.

SOMETHING HERE IS AFFECTING IT.

AT LEAST WE'RE BEING TREATED NICELY.

BUT, MOM, I'M GETTING A BAD TINGLY FEELING ABOUT THIS PLACE. WE SHOULD GO.

NAVIN'S RIGHT, MOM.

YOU SHOULD AT LEAST TRY TO APPLY YOURSELF HERE AND NOT BE SO QUICK TO JUDGE.

DEFEATING THE ELF KING IS THE ONLY WAY WE'RE GOING TO MAKE OUR WAY HOME, RIGHT?

YOU JUST HAVE TO BE WILLING TO FOLLOW THEIR SYSTEM AND DO WHAT YOU CAN TO MAKE THINGS RIGHT.

AS LONG AS YOU'RE DOING WHAT'S RIGHT, THINGS SHOULD WORK THEMSELVES OUT.

AND YOU MIGHT EVEN HELP THE PEOPLE AROUND YOU ALONG THE WAY.

CONSIDERING OUR SITUATION, I DON'T THINK I HAVE MUCH OF A CHOICE, MOM.

COME HERE.

WE'LL BE ALL RIGHT.

WE'LL BE FINE AS LONG AS WE STAY TOGETHER.

WAS IT ALWAYS LIKE THIS, CHIEF?

WELL, THIS IS PRETTY DISAPPOINTING.

THE PLACE IS LIKE A GHOST TOWN.

NO.

IT IS STRANGELY QUIET NOW.

THIS USED TO BE ONE OF THE BUSIEST STREETS.

LET'S FIND SOMETHING TO EAT. I'M FAMISHED.

THIS PLACE LOOKS OPEN.

THIS PLACE IS CLOSED --

-- TO US.

RIGHT?!

ENZO!

I DIDN'T WANT YOUR ROTTEN FOOD, ANYWAY!

IT SMELLS HORRIBLE IN HERE!

I CAN'T BELIEVE I WAS NAIVE ENOUGH TO THINK LIFE COULD BE BETTER HERE.

THE FOOD ACTUALLY SMELLED PRETTY GOOD.

SIGH.

IT ISN'T LIKE THE PEOPLE OF CIELIS TO BEHAVE THIS WAY.

SOMETHING IS WRONG.

GET OVER IT, REDBEARD.

AS LONG AS WE LOOK DIFFERENT, THINGS AREN'T GOING TO CHANGE.

SIR?

EXCUSE ME, SIR?

YOU'RE NOT A GHOST...

A GHOST!

IS THIS A JOKE?

YOU'RE LOOKING FOR A PLACE TO EAT.

PLEASE, COME WITH ME.

YOUR FRIENDS AS WELL.

WHERE ARE YOU GOING, CHIEF?

SOMETHING STRANGE IS GOING ON HERE.

MAYBE THIS GIRL CAN PROVIDE US WITH ANSWERS.

AND MAYBE SOME FOOD?

HMM.

THIS WAY!

CHARLIE'S CAFE

IN HERE!

HEY, WAIT.

I NEED TO TALK WITH YOU.

HELLO?

HELLO?

ANOTHER EMPTY HOLE-IN-THE-WALL.

LOOKS LIKE BUSINESS IS SLOW IN THIS CITY.

CREAK!

SEE, MOM?

I BROUGHT YOU SOME CUSTOMERS.

HELLO, MA'AM.

HELLO.

JUST TAKE A SEAT ANY-WHERE.

MY MOM MAKES THE BEST YUKMO PIES!

CAN I TALK TO YOU IN PRIVATE?

MOM, IT'S OKAY.

WE'RE NOT WELCOME HERE, EITHER.

I'M SO HUNGRY I COULD EAT TWO WHOLE YUKMOS.

I DON'T BELIEVE THE PROBLEM HERE IS WHAT YOU THINK IT IS, ENZO.

YOU CAN DENY IT ALL YOU WANT, CHIEF.

BUT YOU CAN'T CHANGE ANYTHING.

CREAK

WHAT DID I TELL YOU ABOUT BRINGING STRANGERS HERE?

BUT, DAD --

THEY'RE NOT LIKE THE OTHERS.

YOU CAN TELL.

IF WE COULD JUST BOTHER YOU FOR A BIT OF FOOD, WE CAN BE OUT OF YOUR HAIR IN NO TIME.

YOU NEED TO LEAVE HERE FOR YOUR OWN SAFETY.

THIS TOWN IS CURSED.

IF YOU STAY, THEY WILL LOCK YOU UP AND KILL YOU LIKE THE OTHERS.

WHO WILL LOCK US UP?

THE ELF KING?

NO.

THE GUARDIAN COUNCIL.

THE COUNCIL?

THEY WERE THE ONES WHO SENT ME ON THIS MISSION.

HOW MANY YEARS AGO?

THE COUNCIL IS NO LONGER WHAT IT ONCE WAS.

CLICK

THE DOOR IS LOCKED.

47

BUT, DAD, THE COUNCIL ISN'T REAL.

THEY'RE GHOSTS, JUST LIKE THE ONES THAT HAUNT THE CITY!

WHAT ARE THESE GHOSTS YOU'RE TALKING ABOUT, KID?

A FEW YEARS AGO, I SAW A GROUP OF PEOPLE I RECOGNIZED, BUT THEY ACTED LIKE STRANGERS.

THEY TOOK OVER THE CITY IN A MATTER OF DAYS.

AND WHAT MAKES YOU BELIEVE THEY'RE GHOSTS?

LIKE I SAID, I RECOGNIZED THEM.

BUT THESE PEOPLE --

-- THEY'RE SUPPOSED TO BE DEAD.

THAT'S ENOUGH!

REMEMBER WHAT WE TALKED ABOUT?

BUT, DAD --

I CAN'T JUST BOTTLE UP THE TRUTH.

MY PARENTS ARE AFRAID BECAUSE THEY KNOW WE'RE ALWAYS BEING WATCHED!

BUT I DON'T CARE!

ALYSON!

YOU'RE NOT GHOSTS.

AND YOU'RE NOT FROM HERE.

SO YOU MUST BE HERE TO HELP US, RIGHT?

I--

LISTEN, KID.

THE TRUTH IS, WE CAME HERE LOOKING FOR HELP.

NOT THE OTHER WAY AROUND.

SORRY TO DISAPPOINT YOU.

KNOCK KNOCK KNOCK

MENU

IT'S THE GUARD.

IS THERE SOMEPLACE WE CAN HIDE?

NO.

DAD!

WE HAVE TO HELP THEM!

THERE'S NO USE HIDING HERE.

THE GUARD WILL FIND THEM QUICKLY.

THEY CAN ESCAPE THROUGH THE KITCHEN.

THE GUARD IS GOING TO TRY AND TAKE US, TOO.

SO I WANT YOU TO GO WITH YOUR FRIENDS.

WHAT ABOUT YOU AND MOM?

WE'LL BE FINE.

WE CAN STAY HERE AND DISTRACT THEM.

PLEASE TAKE CARE OF ALY.

SHE IS EVERYTHING TO US.

ALY'S INSTINCTS HAVE RARELY BEEN WRONG.

SO I HOPE SHE'S RIGHT AND YOU MANAGE TO HELP US ALL.

I'LL SEE WHAT I CAN DO.

LET'S GO!

THIS WAY!

HURRY!

I'M RIGHT BEHIND YOU, REDBEARD!

OOF!

ERGH!

JUMP! I'LL CATCH YOU!

ERGH!!

POP!

OOF!

NICE CATCH, CHIEF.

YOU OKAY?

I'M FINE.

WE'LL BE SAFER TAKING THE BACKSTREETS.

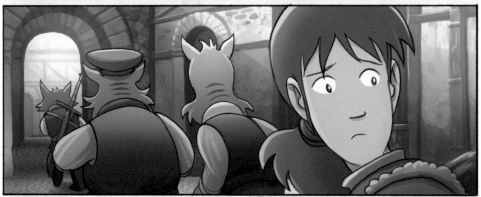

KNOCK KNOCK! KNOCK!

SHK!

COLE?

LET US GO!!

ERGH!

THEY KNOW, SIR.

BUY ME MORE TIME, DUNCAN.

I NEED SOME MORE TIME.

ALY,

BEFORE WE GO ANY FURTHER, I NEED YOU TO SHOW US THE WAY TO THE PRISON.

THE PRISON'S WHAT YOU'RE TRYING TO AVOID!

WHY WOULD YOU WANT TO GO THERE?

BECAUSE WE'RE GOING TO NEED A LITTLE HELP FROM OUR FRIENDS.

HEY! OVER HERE!

HELLP!

HMM.

MISKIT!

GET DOWN AND STAY QUIET!

ARE YOU CRAZY?!

IT'S A HEMLOCK SHIP!

THEY'RE PIRATES!

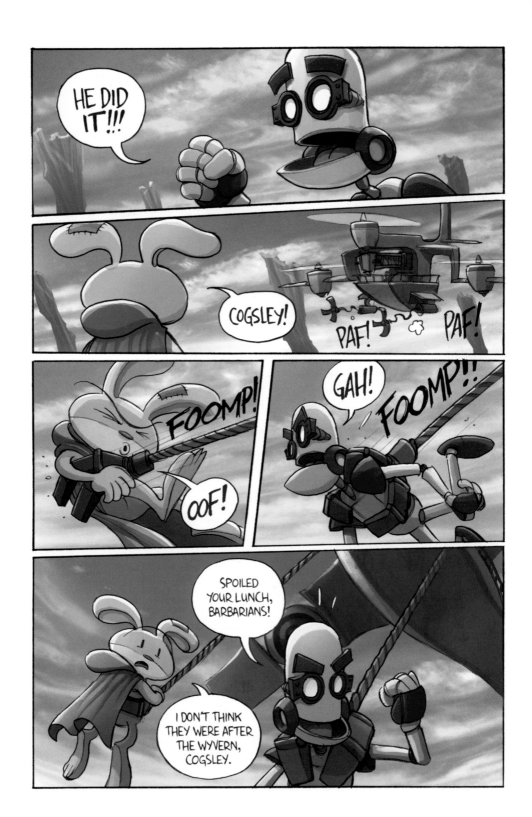

WHIRRRRR

K-CHUNG!

UNGH!

HM.

VERY INTERESTING.

YOU'RE AN OLDER MODEL.

HEY, YOU'RE NOT EXACTLY A SPRING CHICKEN, EITHER!

WELCOME BACK HOME, SIR!

CECIL, WE HAVE A COUPLE OF NEW RECRUITS.

LOAD UP THEIR MEMORY WITH A CLEANING PROGRAM.

YES, SIR!

HEY! NOBODY'S LOADING ANYTHING INTO OUR BRAINS!

DON'T WORRY, MY FRIEND. IT'S A GOOD PROGRAM. IT WILL LET YOU KNOW WHAT NEEDS TO GET DONE AROUND HERE.

AND IT WAS WRITTEN BY YOUR MASTER SILAS.

YOU KNEW SILAS?

CECIL, REFUEL THE SHIP AND SHOW OUR NEW FRIENDS TO THE HOUSE.

YES, SIR.

CHK! CHK! CHK!

UH-OH.

LOOK, KID, I KNOW IT'S DIFFICULT TO SAY GOOD-BYE, SO I'M GOING TO GIVE YOU SOMETHING TO REMEMBER ME BY.

HERE. TAKE THIS STICK.

IT'S BEEN FUN, KID.

GOOD LUCK WITH YOUR LIFE!

THIS WAY, PLEASE.

YOU MENTIONED SILAS.

HOW DID YOU KNOW HIM?

WE SERVED TOGETHER ON THE GUARDIAN COUNCIL.

HE LEFT ME THIS.

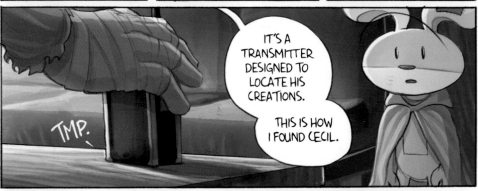

TMP.

IT'S A TRANSMITTER DESIGNED TO LOCATE HIS CREATIONS.

THIS IS HOW I FOUND CECIL.

THE DEVICE SAT QUIETLY FOR YEARS BEFORE IT BEGAN TRANSMITTING ANOTHER SIGNAL.

AND THAT'S HOW I FOUND YOU.

I NEVER GOT TO ASK SILAS WHY HE GAVE ME THIS TRANSMITTER.

IT WAS LONG AFTER OUR TIME ON THE COUNCIL WHEN I LEARNED WHAT IT WAS FOR.

SILAS SAID HE WAS EXILED FROM CIELIS FOR TELLING THE TRUTH.

INTERESTING.

WHY WERE YOU BOOTED OUT?

I WASN'T BOOTED OUT.

I LEFT.

YOU MUST UNDERSTAND THAT SILAS WAS AN ODD MAN.

HE SPOKE HIS MIND FREELY, AND IT WOULD UPSET THE OTHER COUNCIL MEMBERS.

HE WAS EVENTUALLY VOTED OFF THE COUNCIL.

BUT WHAT WOULD PROMPT THE COUNCIL TO EXILE HIM?

HE WANTED TO DESTROY THE MOTHER STONE.

THE MOTHER STONE?

IT IS WHERE ALL OF THESE COME FROM.

OUR STONE-KEEPER POWERS ORIGINATED FROM A SINGLE SOURCE.

CUT FROM A GEM...

...THAT WAS DISCOVERED BY THE EARLY SETTLERS OF THIS PLANET.

REALIZING THAT THE MOTHER STONE CONTAINED TREMENDOUS ENERGY, THE SETTLERS BURIED IT DEEP BENEATH THEIR FIRST CITY...

...CIELIS, THE ANCIENT CAPITAL OF WINDSOR.

THE ORIGINAL GUARDIAN COUNCIL WAS CREATED TO GOVERN USE OF THE MOTHER STONE. SMALL BITS OF THE POWERFUL GEM WERE CUT AND PROVIDED TO THE EARLY SETTLERS OF ALLEDIA TO HELP THEM DEVELOP OUR WORLD.

CENTURIES PASSED, AND HUNDREDS OF STONEKEEPERS WERE BORN. WITH THEIR POWERS THEY BUILT THE FOUNDATION FOR THE GREAT NATIONS OF ALLEDIA, AND ACCELERATED THE DEVELOPMENT OF CITIES ACROSS THE GLOBE.

OF COURSE, MORE THAN A FEW STONEKEEPERS ABUSED THE IMMENSE POWER THAT THE STONES PROVIDED THEM, AND WAGED WAR ON OTHER STONEKEEPERS FOR CONTROL OF THE NATIONS. MANY STONEKEEPERS PERISHED IN THESE BATTLES, AND THEIR STONES PERISHED WITH THEM.

BY THE TIME I HAD JOINED THE COUNCIL, ONLY A SMALL SHARD OF THE STONE REMAINED. IT WAS DECIDED THAT CUTTING THE FINAL PIECE WOULD ONLY BE CONSIDERED IF THE COUNCIL NEEDED TO CALL ON ITS POWERS TO HELP DEFEND CIELIS AND THE NATION OF WINDSOR. IT WAS CONSIDERED A LAST RESORT.

YOUR MASTER SILAS FELT THAT IF WE WERE NOT GOING TO USE THE STONE IMMEDIATELY, WE SHOULD DESTROY IT BEFORE IT FELL INTO THE WRONG HANDS.

TO TREAT IT AS AN INSURANCE POLICY, HE REASONED, WAS A DANGEROUS MISTAKE.

HE CRITICIZED THE COUNCIL FOR MAKING DECISIONS BASED ON ITS FEARS, AND HE BELIEVED THAT IF WE CONTINUED DOWN THIS PATH, WE WOULD SEE OUR FEARS REALIZED.

AT THE TIME, I WAS THE YOUNGEST MEMBER OF THE COUNCIL.

AND DUE TO MY INEXPERIENCE, I MADE SOME DECISIONS THAT I WOULD REGRET FOR THE REST OF MY LIFE.

THE FIRST SUCH DECISION WAS TO VOTE IN
FAVOR OF REMOVING SILAS FROM THE COUNCIL.

SHORTLY THEREAFTER, THE ELVES
UNLEASHED A DEVASTATING ATTACK ON
CIELIS AND FORCED THE COUNCIL TO HIDE
THE CITY IN THE CLOUDS.

SSSIP.

AND THEN I
BEGAN TO SEE
WHAT SILAS SAW.

THE COUNCIL'S
EVERY MOVE WAS
MOTIVATED BY FEAR
AND I WAS JUST TOO
YOUNG TO NOTICE
IT BEFORE.

I COULD NO
LONGER BE A PART
OF THEM.

AND YOU
JUST... LEFT?

SO I TENDERED
MY RESIGNATION.

I BEGAN TO WORK OUTSIDE THE SYSTEM.

I PASSED THE STONE DOWN TO MY SON, AND I TRAINED HIM TO BECOME A BETTER STONEKEEPER THAN I EVER WAS.

HE WAS EAGER TO FIGHT, SO HE SET OUT TO TAKE ON THE ELF KING.

AND WHAT HAPPENED?

THAT'S A STORY FOR ANOTHER TIME.

NOW IF YOU'LL EXCUSE ME...

I HAVE A SUNSET TO CATCH.

YOU'RE WELCOME TO STAY HERE AS LONG AS YOU'D LIKE.

BUT IF YOU WOULD PREFER TO LEAVE, WE CAN PROVIDE YOU WITH A BOAT.

GREAT! WHERE ARE THE PADDLES?

WHAT HAPPENED TO HIS SON?

HE WAS KILLED AND THE STONE RETURNED TO VIGO.

VIGO HASN'T BEEN THE SAME SINCE.

YOU SHOULD KNOW THAT MASTER SILAS IS DEAD.

KILLED BY THE ELVES?

NO. AN ILLNESS.

I'M SORRY TO HEAR THAT.

YOU SHOULD ALSO KNOW THAT HE PASSED HIS POWER DOWN TO HIS GREAT-GRANDDAUGHTER.

HER NAME IS EMILY HAYES, AND SHE COULD USE YOUR HELP RIGHT NOW.

SHE'S SEARCHING FOR CIELIS AND THE GUARDIAN COUNCIL.

SHE'S LOOKING FOR OTHER STONE-KEEPERS LIKE YOU.

I JUST WANTED YOU TO KNOW THAT THERE ARE STILL PEOPLE OUT THERE FIGHTING FOR THE SAME THINGS YOU AND SILAS BELIEVED IN.

EVEN IF YOU'VE LOST FAITH IN THEM.

THANK YOU FOR TELLING ME ABOUT SILAS.

YOU SHOULD LEAVE NOW, BEFORE IT GETS DARK.

IS HE COMING?

NO.

LET'S GO.

AT LEAST WE HAVE ONE NEW ALLY.

ALTHOUGH I'M PRETTY SURE HE HAS NO IDEA WHAT HE'S GETTING HIMSELF INTO.

THE SHIP IS FUELED AND THE SUPPLIES ARE LOADED.

WHAT DO YOU THINK, CECIL?

I THINK IT'S HIGH TIME YOU GOT BACK IN THE GAME, SIR.

OF COURSE YOU DO.

THIS IS WHAT I GET FOR LISTENING TO THE TOYS OF A MADMAN.

Miriam Light

Daniel Light

POOMF!
POOMF!

GAH!

OOF!

THERE HAS TO BE A BETTER WAY TO DO THIS.

SORRY ABOUT THAT, FRIENDS.

BUT I THOUGHT YOU COULD USE A LIFT.

CIELIS HAS BEEN LOST FOR YEARS, AND NO ONE SEEMS TO KNOW IF IT STILL EXISTS.

HOW DO YOU INTEND TO FIND IT?

MY STONE WILL GUIDE US THERE.

THE PATH TO THE CITY IS OPEN TO ALL MEMBERS OF THE GUARDIAN COUNCIL, PAST AND PRESENT.

SO LONG AS YOU'RE WILLING TO ENTER THE EYE OF THE STORM.

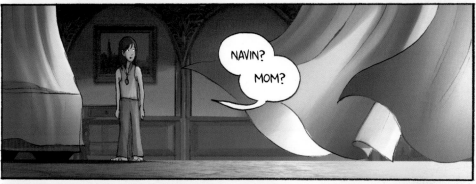

WELCOME TO THE GARDEN OF THE KEEPERS.

THIS WILL BE THE NEXUS FOR THE COUNCIL'S SERIES OF TESTS.

YOU WILL MEET YOUR FELLOW STUDENTS HERE.

KSH!

THE COUNCIL WILL BE WITH YOU SHORTLY.

GOOD
LUCK.

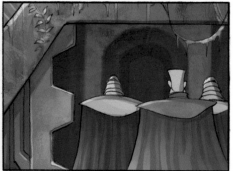

98

I SHOULD SERIOUSLY KILL YOU RIGHT NOW, GRIFFIN!

STOP!

YOU DON'T WANT BLOOD ON YOUR HANDS, PIERCE.

LEAVE HIM ALONE.

YOU KNOW THIS CREEP DESERVES IT, RONIN!

MAYBE SO --

-- BUT WE SHOULD LET THE VOID DETERMINE HIS FATE.

YOU'RE GONNA GET WHAT YOU DESERVE, GRIFFIN.

MAYBE NOT NOW, BUT SOON.

AND YOU MUST BE THE NEW KID.

MY NAME IS EMILY.

EMILY HAYES.

MY NAME IS RONIN.

AND THIS IS PIERCE.

HEY.

WHAT DID MAX TELL YOU?

THAT YOU'RE THE "CHOSEN ONE" HERE TO SAVE CIELIS?

'CAUSE THAT'S WHAT HE TOLD THE REST OF US.

HE TOLD ME I WOULD BE TESTED.

AND DID HE TELL YOU ABOUT THE CONSEQUENCES FOR FAILING THESE "TESTS"?

YOU DON'T JUST GET TO WALK OUT OF HERE, EMILY.

STONEKEEPERS ARE BROUGHT HERE TO DIE.

STOP SCARING HER, PIERCE.

I'M NOT SCARED.

I WANT TO KNOW EVERYTHING.

HOW MANY STONEKEEPERS ARE HERE WITH US?

WHEN THE TESTS BEGAN, THERE WERE AT LEAST THIRTY KEEPERS.

NOW THERE ARE ONLY A SMALL HANDFUL LEFT.

WHAT HAPPENED TO THE OTHERS?

DID YOU NOTICE THE PRETTY STATUES?

WHEN YOU DIE IN THE VOID, YOU GET TURNED TO STONE.

THE VOID?

BWAAAAAAH

WHAT WAS THAT?

THE COUNCIL.

THE TESTS ARE ABOUT TO BEGIN.

WE NEED TO MEET IN THE CENTER. FOLLOW US.

YOU COMING?

YEAH, I'LL BE RIGHT BEHIND YOU.

RONIN, WHAT IS THE VOID?

THE VOID IS A SIMULATION.

IT'S A VIRTUAL SPACE WHERE THE COUNCIL SENDS US TO BE TESTED.

THIS WEEK'S TESTS ARE TO BE THE FINAL ONES.

WHOEVER SURVIVES THEM WILL JOIN THE COUNCIL.

AWW, NO.

LOOK WHO'S STILL HERE.

PIERCE!

GLAD TO SEE YOU'RE STILL WITH US!

I FIGURED YOU GUYS WERE TOAST!

SORRY YOUR BUDDY BIT THE DUST, PIERCE.

BUT HE WASN'T STRONG ENOUGH TO BE HERE TO BEGIN WITH.

JAMES WAS MY BEST FRIEND.

WHAT PART OF "SURVIVAL OF THE FITTEST" DO YOU NOT UNDERSTAND?

I HOPE YOU REALIZE I'M NOT GOING TO LET YOU GET OUT OF THIS UNSCATHED.

PIERCE.

I KNOW, I KNOW.

SAVE IT FOR THE VOID.

ISN'T THIS A LAST-MAN-STANDING AFFAIR?

RONIN CAN BE THE LAST ONE STANDING WITH ME.

FIND ME IN THE VOID AND WE'LL SEE WHO'S THE LAST ONE STANDING.

WE FIGHT EACH OTHER?

WE DO WHATEVER IT TAKES TO SURVIVE.

YOU HEAR THAT, SHRIMP?

NO ONE WANTS YOU ON THEIR SIDE.

WHO BROUGHT THE LITTLE TRAITOR?

AND WHY IS HE EVEN STILL ALIVE?

SHOVE!

LOOKS LIKE THE COUNCIL DECIDED TO ABANDON HIM.

THAT MEANS THE MOMENT YOU STEP INTO THE VOID...

...YOU'RE AS GOOD AS STONE.

HERE THEY COME!

STONEKEEPERS.

WELCOME TO YOUR FINAL DAYS OF TESTING.

108

PST!

OVER HERE!

MAX?

KEEP IT DOWN AND COME OVER HERE.

GET DOWN! DOWN!

WHAT ARE WE HIDING FROM?

SHH.

KRRKKRKKk

KRRKr

I THINK IT'S GONE NOW.

WHAT WAS IT?

A GROUL.

THEY WERE USED BY THE OLD COUNCILS TO GUARD THEIR MOST VALUABLE TREASURES.

I DIDN'T REALIZE THEY STILL EXISTED.

WHAT ARE THEY GUARDING HERE?

THAT'S A GOOD QUESTION.

I DON'T KNOW.

COME ON, WE BETTER GO FIND THE OTHERS.

I'D RATHER NOT, IF YOU KNOW WHAT I MEAN.

WHY DO THEY HAVE IT OUT FOR YOU?

I GUESS I DIDN'T TELL THEM THE WHOLE TRUTH.

I DIDN'T TELL THEM WHAT IT WOULD BE LIKE HERE.

WHAT WERE THEY EXPECTING?

A REGULAR SCHOOL?

NOT EVERYONE IS AS RESILIENT AS YOU ARE, EMILY.

THEY AREN'T AS WILLING TO FACE DIFFICULT CHALLENGES.

IT'S WHAT MAKES YOU SPECIAL.

WELL, THE ONE THING I LEARNED ABOUT DIFFICULT CHALLENGES IS THAT YOU DON'T WANT TO FACE THEM ALONE.

WE'RE GOING TO NEED THE OTHERS' HELP WHETHER YOU LIKE IT OR NOT.

AND DON'T FLATTER ME.

IT MAKES ME FEEL WEIRD.

OW.

I CUT MYSELF.

ARE YOU OKAY?

I'M FINE, BUT--

-- YOU'RE NOT SUPPOSED TO BLEED IN THE VOID.

MAYBE IT'S PART OF THE TEST?

NO.

SOMETHING'S NOT RIGHT.

WAIT A MINUTE.

I KNOW THIS PLACE.

I'VE BEEN HERE BEFORE.

I'M CERTAIN OF IT.

SZRAK!

EMILY, WAIT!

WALK AWAY, ZAREN!

YOU DON'T HAVE TO DO THIS.

WE CAN BOTH LIVE TO FIGHT A LITTLE LONGER.

JUST WALK AWAY.

WHY DELAY THE INEVITABLE, PIERCE?

LET'S FINISH THIS.

RIGHT HERE. RIGHT NOW.

WE NEED TO STOP THEM FROM KILLING EACH OTHER.

MAX!

I'M NOT GOING TO PLAY THIS GAME!

WE NEED TO FIND A WAY OUT OF THIS!

IF THEY FINISH EACH OTHER OFF, WE WON'T HAVE TO.

R-RIGHT.

FASH!

SHWIK!!!

URK!!

LEAVE MY FRIENDS ALONE.

THIS IS NONE OF YOUR BUSINESS!

WHAT PART OF "SURVIVAL OF THE FITTEST" DO YOU NOT UNDERSTAND?

CHUCK!

DO SOMETHING!

SHE'S -- SHE'S TOO STRONG.

YOU'RE USELESS!

IF I LET YOU DOWN, WILL YOU BEHAVE?

OKAY! OKAY!

NOW APOLOGIZE TO MY FRIENDS.

I'M SORRY!

SORRY!!

WHUMP!!

NICE GOING, HAYES!

NOW FOR SOME UNFINISHED BUSINESS.

PIERCE, WAIT.

I CAN HELP YOU.

IT'S A LITTLE LATE FOR THAT, GRIFFIN.

WAIT! YOU HAVE TO LISTEN TO ME!

LISTENING TO YOU IS WHAT GOT US HERE IN THE FIRST PLACE!

BUT I'M ON YOUR SIDE!

LET HIM TALK, PIERCE.

YOU DON'T KNOW WHAT THIS WEASEL IS CAPABLE OF.

HE LIED TO US AND LEFT US FOR DEAD.

WE'RE LUCKY HE GOT DROPPED IN THE VOID WITH US SO WE CAN GET OUR REVENGE.

BUT WE'RE NOT IN THE VOID.

THAT'S WHAT I WANTED TO TELL YOU.

WE'RE IN THE CATACOMBS BENEATH CIELIS.

IT'S A REAL PLACE, AND I KNOW HOW TO GET US OUT OF HERE.

YOU'RE LYING.

WE DON'T BLEED IN THE VOID, RIGHT?

BUT LOOK AT YOUR NOSE.

I DON'T KNOW WHAT GAME YOU'RE PLAYING, GRIFFIN,

BUT I'D RATHER GET RID OF YOU BEFORE WE ALL FIND OUT.

KKRKKRKKK

WHAT WAS THAT?

THE REAL THREAT.

WE SHOULD GET TO HIGH GROUND.

NOW.

DRIP

HUH?

DRIP

DRIP

DRIP

121

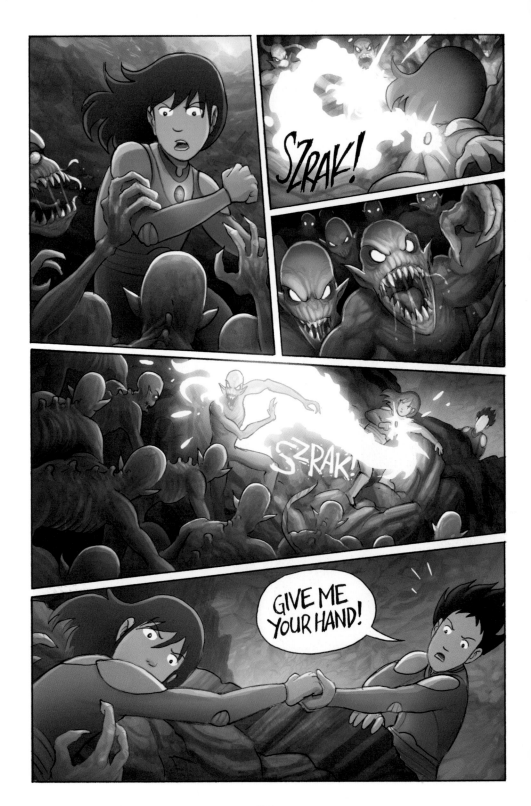

EMILY! OVER HERE!

WHERE ARE WE, MAX?

THIS IS THE CISTERN.

IT'S WHERE THE CITY'S WATER SUPPLY COMES FROM.

WHAT ABOUT THE GROULS?

WHY AREN'T THEY FOLLOWING US DOWN HERE?

THEY CAN'T SWIM.

WHAT NOW, GRIFFIN?

I'LL TAKE US TO THE EXIT.

HOW CAN WE BE SURE YOU'RE TELLING THE TRUTH?

LOOK, I'M ONLY TRYING TO HELP.

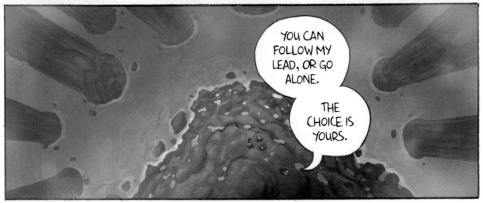

YOU CAN FOLLOW MY LEAD, OR GO ALONE.

THE CHOICE IS YOURS.

YEARS AGO, I DESIGNED YARBORO PENITENTIARY, BUT IT WAS ONLY AFTER THE BUILDING WAS COMPLETE THAT I REALIZED I HAD MADE A MISTAKE.

I FOUND A SIMPLE DESIGN FLAW THAT WOULD COMPROMISE THE INSTITUTION'S SECURITY.

NOW IMAGINE MY SURPRISE TO SEE THAT THIS FLAW CAN SERVE A GOOD PURPOSE.

EVEN WHEN YOU DON'T KNOW WHAT YOU'RE DOING, YOU KIND OF DO, I GUESS.

THAT'S THE ENTRY POINT. IT'S A GRATE WITH BLIND SPOTS ON ALL SIDES.

NO ONE WILL SEE YOU THERE.

TAP!

THANK YOU, MA'AM. FOR THE LODGING, AS WELL.

THANKS, MRS. PINE, FOR EVERYTHING.

DON'T YOU WORRY ABOUT IT.

ALY, WE DON'T HAVE MANY YOUNG FIGHTERS LEFT IN THIS TOWN, SO PLEASE...

...STAY SAFE.

ANOTHER BATCH OF PRISONERS, AND NONE OF THEM LOOK LIKE CRIMINALS.

THIS PLACE HAS GONE LOOPY, CHIEF.

AT THIS RATE, THE WHOLE CITY WILL BE UNDER ARREST IN A WEEK!

I HAVEN'T SEEN THE GUARD SO ACTIVE BEFORE.

THEY MUST BE PLANNING SOMETHING.

LET'S MOVE BEFORE WE FIND OUT WHAT IT IS.

THE GRATE LOOKS A LITTLE TIGHT.

WHY ARE YOU LOOKING AT ME LIKE THAT?!

ALY AND I WILL GO ON OUR OWN.

ENZO, YOU STAND WATCH.

I'M LOOKING FOR ELVES, RIGHT?

YOU'LL PROBABLY SMELL 'EM FIRST!

ALY?

MR. PETERS?

ALY, IT IS YOU!

I -- I DON'T KNOW WHY I WAS PUT IN HERE!

I HAVEN'T DONE ANYTHING WRONG!

DON'T WORRY.

WE'LL GET YOU OUT.

BUT WE NEED TO FIND SOME FRIENDS WHO CAN HELP US.

HAVE YOU SEEN ANY ELVES BEING BROUGHT IN HERE?

I HEARD ABOUT TWO ELVES BEING HELD IN CELL BLOCK FOUR.

BUT, ALY, WHY ARE YOU DEALING WITH ELVES?

LET'S GO.

AND WHO IS THIS HALF-BREED?!

ALY!

YOU MUSTN'T TRUST THEM!

TRUST NO ONE!!

THE PEOPLE OF CIELIS ARE STRICKEN WITH FEAR.

IT CLOUDS THEIR JUDGMENT AND MAKES THEM DIFFICULT TO DEAL WITH.

THAT MEANS WE LEAVE THE OTHERS HERE UNTIL WE CAN RESOLVE THINGS WITH THE COUNCIL.

UNDERSTAND?

I UNDERSTAND.

LEON!

I FOUND THEM!

SO THINGS DIDN'T QUITE GO ACCORDING TO PLAN.

LEON!

THIS CITY IS AS CORRUPT AS MY HOMELAND.

IF THIS WAS YOUR LAST HOPE, I'D SAY WE'RE ALL IN DEEP TROUBLE.

YOU'RE RIGHT.

THE GUARDIAN COUNCIL HAS BEEN COMPROMISED.

IN ORDER TO SET THINGS RIGHT, I WILL NEED YOUR HELP.

HOLD STILL.

SHING!

NOW GET OUT OF THERE.

YOU TRUST ME OVER YOUR OWN SUPERIORS.

WHY?

142

WE WERE SEPARATED ON THE LANDING DOCK, JUST AFTER WE LOST YOU.

SHE'S AT THE ACADEMY NOW.

TRELLIS BELIEVES THE ELF KING HAS SOMETHING TO DO WITH THIS.

HE'S IN THE CITY.

I CAN FEEL IT.

ALY!

MOM! DAD!

ALY!

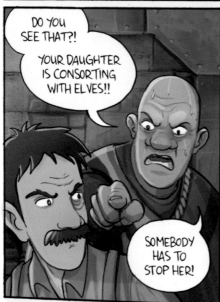

LEON, THERE ARE TOO MANY OF THEM.

IF WE KNOCK OUT THE CAPTAIN, WE MIGHT HAVE A CHANCE.

JUST FOLLOW MY LEAD.

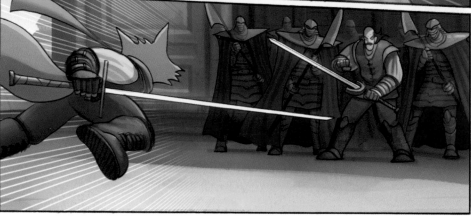

KRSH!

WE'LL HAVE TO DO SOME PUNCHING, TOO.

SHIRK!

YOU READY?

VRRRRRN!

LEON! TRELLIS!

LOOK OUT BEHIND YOU!

SZPAK!

FWOOM!

STONE AGAIN. IT'S A CURSE, ISN'T IT?

YOU SHOULD HAVE SEEN THIS COMING FROM A MILE AWAY.

ONE OF THE OLDEST TRICKS IN THE BOOK.

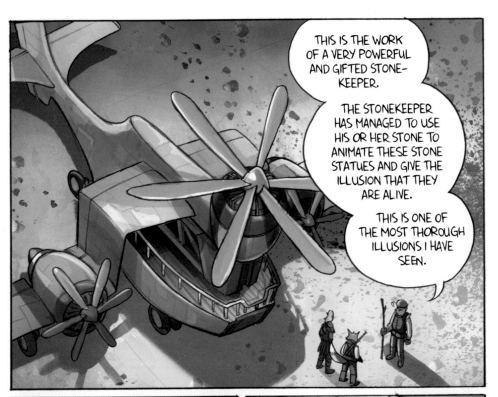

THIS IS THE WORK OF A VERY POWERFUL AND GIFTED STONE-KEEPER.

THE STONEKEEPER HAS MANAGED TO USE HIS OR HER STONE TO ANIMATE THESE STONE STATUES AND GIVE THE ILLUSION THAT THEY ARE ALIVE.

THIS IS ONE OF THE MOST THOROUGH ILLUSIONS I HAVE SEEN.

IF IT WAS SO THOROUGH, THEN WHY DID THE STATUES BREAK APART SO EASILY?

THE ILLUSION'S STRENGTH DEPENDS ON BOTH THE SKILL AND THE PROXIMITY OF THE KEEPER WHO CASTS IT.

IT IS LIKELY THE STONEKEEPER IS FAR AWAY FROM HERE.

SILAS USED TO SAY THAT HIS DISTANCE SPELLS RARELY WORKED WHILE HE WAS UNDERGROUND.

UNDERGROUND.

OF COURSE.

WHERE DID YOU SAY EMILY WENT?

TO THE ACADEMY.

THE ACADEMY...

THE MOTHER STONE, SIR.

WE MUST GET TO EMILY, QUICKLY.

CECIL, GATHER THE OTHERS.

LET'S GO! WE HAVE NO TIME TO LOSE!

CECIL, WHY DO THE STATUES TAKE THE FORM OF THE DECEASED?

THE POWER TO RE-ANIMATE IS ONE OF THE DARKEST FORMS OF MAGIC THERE IS.

A LARGE AMOUNT OF NEGATIVE ENERGY IS REQUIRED TO KEEP THE ILLUSION ALIVE.

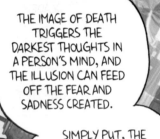

THE IMAGE OF DEATH TRIGGERS THE DARKEST THOUGHTS IN A PERSON'S MIND, AND THE ILLUSION CAN FEED OFF THE FEAR AND SADNESS CREATED.

SIMPLY PUT, THE ILLUSIONS OF THE DEAD ARE STRONGER.

THEN WHOEVER IS CREATING THESE ILLUSIONS MUST NOT CARE VERY MUCH ABOUT OTHER PEOPLE.

UNFORTUNATELY, THAT IS THE MARK OF MANY POWERFUL STONEKEEPERS.

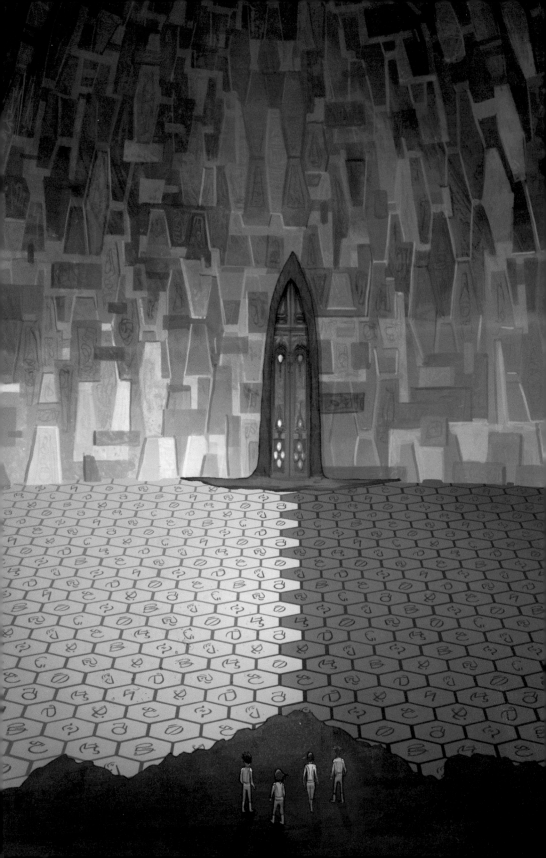

WHAT IS THIS, GRIFFIN?

IT'S AN OLD CIELAN CHILDREN'S GAME.

TWO PLAYERS FOLLOW THE SAME PATH SIMULTANEOUSLY.

WHAT HAPPENS IF YOU STEP ON THE WRONG TILE?

ONE PLAYER TAKES THE LIGHT PATH, AND THE OTHER ONE TAKES THE DARK.

IT MUST BE THE KEY TO OPENING THAT DOOR.

UNGH!

YOU LOSE, APPARENTLY.

AND HOW DO WE KNOW THE PROPER ORDER?

THE MARKINGS ON THE TILES ARE FROM THE OLD CIELAN NUMBER SYSTEM.

THIS DOESN'T LOOK LIKE A PUZZLE AT ALL.

IT IS SIMPLY TELLING US THE CORRECT SEQUENCE OF TILES.

THEN THE CHALLENGE MUST BE TO SEE IF WE CAN WORK TOGETHER.

I FEEL LIKE I JUST SHOWED UP TO A FINAL EXAM I DIDN'T STUDY FOR.

DON'T WORRY, EMILY.

WE'LL BE HERE TO GUIDE YOU THROUGH.

THEY DON'T BELIEVE WE CAN WORK TOGETHER.

THEY THINK WE WOULD RATHER DESTROY EACH OTHER FOR A SPOT ON THE COUNCIL.

I DON'T KNOW ABOUT YOU GUYS, BUT I JUST WANT TO GO HOME.

MAX GOES FIRST.

WHAT?

WANT TO REGAIN OUR TRUST? YOU CAN START RIGHT HERE.

YOU OWE THIS TO US.

RONIN, THE TILE YOU'RE STANDING ON...

...IT'S NOT LIGHTING UP.

EMILY, LISTEN!

THIS IS NOT THE TIME TO HESITATE.

ALL OUR LIVES HANG IN THE BALANCE!

BUT THERE'S SOMETHING WRONG, MAX.

I CAN SENSE IT.

IF YOU MAKE ONE FALSE MOVE, WE ALL DIE.

WE NEED TO TRUST EACH OTHER AND STAY FOCUSED.

EMILY, PLEASE.

LET'S GO HOME.

PLINK

SHAAAA!

MAX, THIS ISN'T THE EXIT.

HOW DO YOU KNOW?

BEFORE I ARRIVED IN CIELIS, MY STONE TOLD ME ABOUT THIS HALLWAY.

IT WARNED ME ABOUT WALKING THROUGH IT.

DID IT TELL YOU WHAT YOU MIGHT FIND AT THE END?

NO.

AND YOU TRUST THE VOICE MORE THAN US?

THERE AREN'T MANY PEOPLE WHO CAN UNDERSTAND WHAT IT'S LIKE TO BE A STONEKEEPER.

THAT'S WHY WE HAVE TO STICK TOGETHER.

COME ON.

WE'RE ALMOST OUT.

FWOOOSH

THERE ARE NO OTHERS.

IT'S JUST YOU AND ME.

180

THE GUARDS HAVE BEEN ORDERED TO KILL YOUR FAMILY IF YOU TRY AND ATTACK ME.

SO HERE IS YOUR CHOICE.

YOU CAN TRY TO STOP ME WHILE YOUR FAMILY IS EXECUTED --

-- OR YOU LET ME WALK OUT OF HERE --

-- AND I SPARE THEIR LIVES.

HOW DO I KNOW YOU'LL KEEP YOUR WORD?

THEY BROUGHT YOU DOWN HERE WITHOUT MAX.

HOW?

THEY USED A THING CALLED A TRANSPORE, JUST BEYOND THE HEXAGON FIELD.

I'LL SHOW YOU.

EMILY --

I SHOULD HAVE LISTENED TO YOU ABOUT THIS PLACE.

I WAS WRONG.

C'MON, MOM --

-- WE NEED TO STAY FOCUSED ON HOW TO SET THINGS RIGHT.

TELL LEN WE'RE IN THE GARDEN.

HAVE THEM MEET US IN FRONT OF THE ACADEMY.

WHO--

YOU'LL HAVE TO DO BETTER THAN THAT, OLD MAN!

SZRAK!

ZWIK

WHO WAS THAT?

THE GHOST OF AN OLD FRIEND.

DID YOU GET THE STONE?

IT WAS ALMOST TOO EASY.

THE KING WILL BE VERY PLEASED.

HOW YOU RECOVER FROM THESE TRIALS IS WHAT REALLY MATTERS.

THE ELF KING HAS NOW BECOME MORE POWERFUL THAN EVER BEFORE.

WE'LL NEED TO PREPARE FOR A LONG BATTLE AHEAD.

HEY, EM,

REMEMBER--

-- YOU'RE NOT ALONE.

WHAT ARE YOU DOING?

A TRIBUTE FOR FALLEN STONEKEEPERS.

CAN I JOIN YOU?

OF COURSE.

ARE WE THE LAST ONES?

DO YOU MEAN STONEKEEPERS?

THERE ARE VERY FEW OF US LEFT, TO BE SURE.

IF MAX IS WORKING WITH THE ELF KING, HE CAN GRANT THE ELVES ACCESS TO THE MOTHER STONE.

THEY'LL BE ABLE TO CREATE A NEW COUNCIL UNDER THEIR CONTROL.

207

BUT WE'RE THE LAST ONES ON OUR SIDE.

WE ARE THE LAST GUARDIAN COUNCIL.

AREN'T WE?

BACK AT THE ACADEMY, YOU ENCOUNTERED THE LIKENESSES OF SEVERAL YOUNG STONEKEEPERS.

AMONG THEM WERE STUDENTS OF MINE, FROM MANY YEARS AGO.

RONIN WAS MY BEST STUDENT.

SHE WAS THE YOUNGEST STONE-KEEPER TO BE OFFERED A PLACE ON THE GUARDIAN COUNCIL.

SHE CHOSE NOT TO JOIN THE COUNCIL, CLAIMING THAT THE RESPONSIBILITY WAS TOO GREAT FOR A PERSON HER AGE.

RONIN WOULD HAVE JOINED A COUNCIL WITH SEVERAL OTHER POWERFUL STONEKEEPERS...

BUT YOU'LL BE JOINED BY AN OLD MAN FAR PAST HIS PRIME, AND WE'LL BE UP AGAINST A VERY POWERFUL ENEMY.

ARE YOU SURE YOU'RE READY FOR THIS KIND OF RESPONSIBILITY?

THE DIFFERENCE BETWEEN HER AND ME IS THAT SHE FELT SHE HAD A CHOICE.

I MAY NOT BE AS CLEVER AS MAX,

OR AS SKILLED AS RONIN...

...BUT DON'T ASK ME IF I'M READY.

BECAUSE NO MATTER WHAT HAPPENS, I'LL HAVE TO BE.

END OF BOOK FOUR

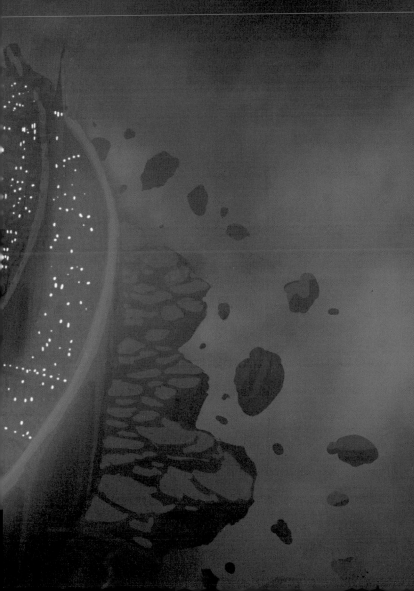

for Julie

CREATED AT

BOLT CITY
P R O D U C T I O N S

IN ALHAMBRA, CALIFORNIA

WRITTEN AND ILLUSTRATED BY
KAZU KIBUISHI

LEAD PRODUCTION ARTIST
JASON CAFFOE

COLORS & BACKGROUND

JASON CAFFOE
ZANE YARBROUGH
KAZU KIBUISHI

PAGE FLATTING

DENVER JACKSON
JON LEE
STUART LIVINGSTON
RIKKI SIMONS
MICHAEL REGINA
KEAN SOO

SPECIAL THANKS

GORDON LUK, AMY KIM KIBUISHI, JUDY HANSEN,
DAVID SAYLOR, PHIL FALCO, CASSANDRA PELHAM,
BEN ZHU & THE GALLERY NUCLEUS CREW, NICK
& MELISSA HARRIS, NANCY CAFFOE, OVERBROOK
ENTERTAINMENT, THE FLIGHT ARTISTS, TAKA
KIBUISHI, TIM GANTER, RACHEL ORMISTON,
KHANG LE & ADHESIVE GAMES, OVI NEDELCU,
TAO AKASHI, JUNE KIBUISHI, SUNNI KIM, ARDEN
KÖPRÜLÜYAN & TUDEM PUBLISHING, SHEILA
MARIE EVERETT, ANTHONY WU, ERIC WU, JEFF
SMITH, STEVE HAMAKER, JENNY ROBB, SCOTT
MCCLOUD, & JUNI.

CATACOMBS OF CIELIS

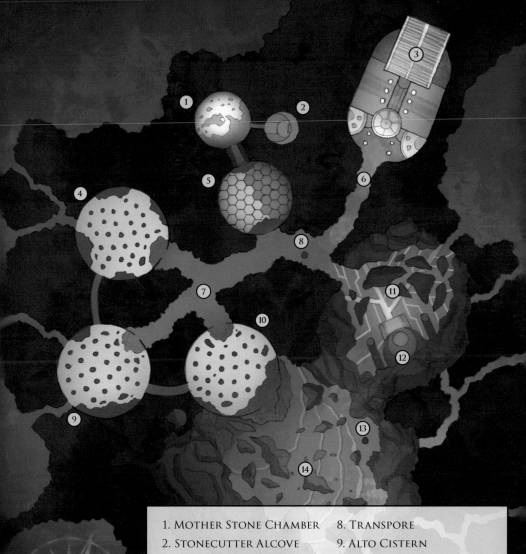

OTHER GRAPHIC NOVELS
BY KAZU KIBUISHI

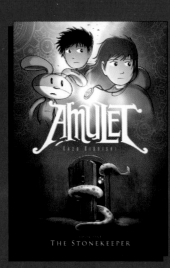

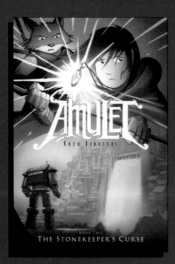

MAP OF CIELIS

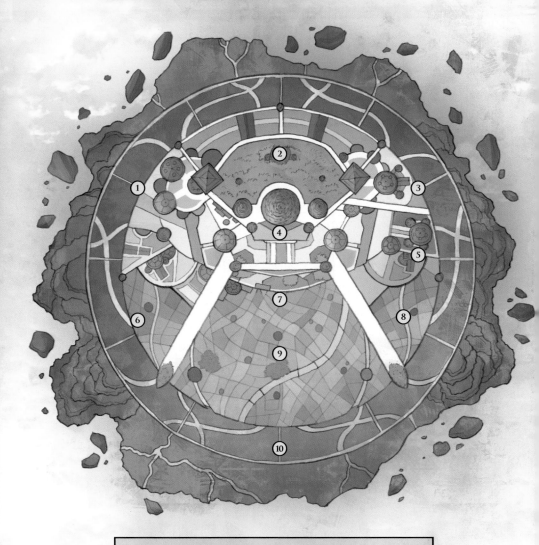

ABOUT THE AUTHOR

Kazu Kibuishi is the founder and editor of the acclaimed Flight anthologies and is also the creator of *Copper*, a collection of his popular webcomic that features an adventuresome boy-and-dog pair. *Amulet, Book One: The Stonekeeper* was an ALA Best Book for Young Adults and a Children's Choice Book Award finalist. The second and third books in the Amulet series, *The Stonekeeper's Curse* and *The Cloud Searchers*, were both *New York Times* bestsellers. Kazu lives and works in Alhambra, California, with his wife and fellow comics artist, Amy Kim Kibuishi, and their son.

Visit Kazu online at www.boltcity.com.